D0505107

LE CORDON BLEU

HOME COLLECTION

·PATISSERIE·

MEREHURST

contents

recipe ratings 🌼 *easy* 🌼🌼 *a little more care needed* 🌼🌼🌼 *more care needed*

Tartelettes amandines

These small almond cakes are a well-loved patisserie classic and are perfect for eating at tea time. Amandine is the name given to various almond-flavoured French pastries and cakes.

*Preparation time **45 minutes***
*Total cooking time **20 minutes***
Makes 18

ALMOND CREAM
115 g (3³/4 oz) unsalted butter, softened
115 g (3³/4 oz) caster sugar
grated rind of 1 lemon
2 eggs, beaten
115 g (3³/4 oz) ground almonds
30 g (1 oz) plain flour
few drops of vanilla extract or essence

1 quantity sweet pastry (see page 59)
125 g (4 oz) seedless raspberry jam
60 g (2 oz) flaked almonds
45 g (1¹/2 oz) apricot jam
45 g (1¹/2 oz) icing sugar, sieved
few drops of pink food colouring

1 To make the almond cream, beat the butter, sugar and lemon rind together using a wooden spoon or electric beaters until light and creamy. Gradually add the eggs, a sixth at a time, beating well between each addition. Stir in the ground almonds, flour and the vanilla extract. Transfer to a piping bag fitted with a 2 cm (³/4 inch) nozzle and refrigerate.

2 Brush eighteen 6 x 2 cm (2¹/2 x ³/4 inch) loose-bottomed tartlet tins with melted butter. Roll out the pastry on a floured surface to a 2 mm (¹/8 inch) thickness. Cut eighteen 10 cm (4 inch) circles of pastry to fit the tins, then ease them into the tins and prick the bases with a fork. Preheat the oven to moderate 180°C (350°F/Gas 4).

3 Beat the raspberry jam with a spoon until soft and fluid, then place a little in the base of each tartlet. Pipe in the almond cream until the tartlets are three quarters full and bake for 12–15 minutes, or until golden. Cool the tartlets in the tins on a wire rack. Toast the flaked almonds under a medium grill until golden, taking care not to burn.

4 In a small pan, heat the apricot jam with 2 tablespoons water. When the mixture has melted and begins to boil, sieve it into a small bowl and, while still hot, brush it over the tartlets. Arrange the toasted almonds over one half of each tartlet.

5 In a small bowl, mix the icing sugar, 2 teaspoons of water and a tiny amount of the pink food colouring until the mixture is smooth and just delicately pink. Spoon the icing thinly over the half of the tartlets without the toasted almonds.

Apple slice

Delicate poached apples and a vanilla pastry cream inside light pastry make this dessert a lovely end to a light lunch or a delicious mid-afternoon snack.

*Preparation time **1 hour 20 minutes**
    + 15 minutes chilling*
*Total cooking time **1 hour 10 minutes***
*Serves **8–10***

POACHED APPLES
500 g (1 lb) Granny Smith apples
grated rind and juice of 1 lemon
250 g (8 oz) sugar
1 cinnamon stick
1/2 vanilla pod, split lengthways

PASTRY CREAM
500 ml (16 fl oz) milk
1/2 vanilla pod, split lengthways
5 egg yolks
125 g (4 oz) caster sugar
2 tablespoons plain flour
2 tablespoons cornflour

**1 quantity sweet pastry (with 1 1/2 teaspoons mixed
   spice added to the flour) (see page 59)**
1 egg, beaten
60 g (2 oz) icing sugar
20 g (3/4 oz) flaked almonds

1 Brush a 34 x 11 cm (14 x 4 1/2 inch) rectangular loose-bottomed tart tin with melted butter and dust with flour.

2 To make the poached apples, peel, halve and core the apples, toss in the lemon juice, then remove and set aside, reserving the juice. Place the lemon rind, juice, sugar, cinnamon stick and vanilla pod into a medium pan with 250 ml (8 fl oz) water and heat gently until the sugar has dissolved. Simmer for 5 minutes, then add the apple halves and poach for 15 minutes, or until

tender. Remove from the syrup and drain on paper towels, reserving the syrup.

3 To make the pastry cream, place the milk and vanilla in a pan and bring slowly to the boil. In a bowl, whisk the egg yolks with the sugar until light in colour. Sieve in the flour and cornflour and whisk until well combined. Remove and discard the vanilla pod, then pour half the boiling milk into the yolk mixture, whisk well and return to the pan with the remaining milk. Bring to the boil, stirring constantly, and boil for 1 minute to completely cook the flour. Remove from the heat and spread the pastry cream on a tray to cool quickly. Cover the surface with baking paper to prevent a skin forming and leave to cool. Once cooled, whisk until smooth.

4 Preheat the oven to moderately hot 200°C (400°F/ Gas 6). Roll out two thirds of the pastry on a floured surface to a 3 mm (1/8 inch) thickness and use it to line the prepared tin, then trim the edges neatly. Half fill with the pastry cream, levelling the surface. Slice the poached apple into about 5 mm (1/4 inch) slices and arrange on top of the pastry cream. Roll out the remaining pastry to a 3 mm (1/8 inch) thickness and cut long strips, 5 mm (1/4 inch) wide. Brush the beaten egg around the top edge of the pastry lining and use the strips to make a diagonal lattice over the apples. Brush the lattice with more egg and chill for 15 minutes.

5 Bake for 35–40 minutes, or until golden, covering the top with foil after 15 minutes to stop it burning. Remove from the oven and cool on a wire rack in the tin.

6 Meanwhile, sieve the icing sugar into a small bowl and mix with enough of the poaching liquid from the apples to form a runny icing. Toast the almonds under a medium grill until golden, taking care not to burn.

7 When the slice is completely cold, remove from the tin and sprinkle with the toasted almonds. Drizzle the top with thin lines of the icing dropped from a teaspoon or fork. To serve, cut into slices with a serrated knife.

Apricot and ginger shortbreads

A trio of complementary textures—poached apricots, crunchy shortbread and creamy mascarpone—ensure the success of these desserts. They can be made ahead of time and put together at the last minute.

*Preparation time **50 minutes + 50 minutes chilling***
*Total cooking time **50 minutes***
Makes 6

GINGER SHORTBREADS
60 g (2 oz) unsalted butter
60 g (2 oz) caster sugar
3/4 teaspoon ground ginger
I egg, beaten
60 g (2 oz) ground almonds
170 g (5¹/2 oz) plain flour
40 g (1¹/4 oz) preserved ginger, drained and finely chopped (reserving at least I tablespoon syrup)

POACHED APRICOTS
200 g (6¹/2 oz) sugar
2 cloves
I star anise
¹/2 vanilla pod, split lengthways
9 fresh apricots

MASCARPONE CREAM
250 g (8 oz) mascarpone cheese
30 g (I oz) icing sugar
I tablespoon syrup from jar of preserved ginger
seeds from ¹/2 vanilla pod, scraped out

icing sugar, to dust

1 To make the ginger shortbreads, butter two baking trays and dust lightly with flour. Using a wooden spoon or electric beaters, cream the butter, sugar and ground ginger together until light and creamy, then gradually add the egg, beating well between additions. Sieve together the ground almonds and flour and stir into the butter and sugar with the preserved ginger to form a soft dough. Cover in plastic wrap and chill for 30 minutes.

2 To make the poached apricots, place the sugar and 410 ml (13 fl oz) water in a medium pan and heat gently until the sugar has dissolved. Add the cloves, star anise and vanilla pod and simmer for 5 minutes. Halve and stone the apricots, add to the liquid and poach for 5–10 minutes, or until just tender to the point of a knife. Remove the apricots to a wire rack to drain, and boil the syrup until reduced by half. Strain, discard the spices and leave to cool.

3 Roll out the shortbread dough between two sheets of baking paper to about a 3 mm (¹/8 inch) thickness. Use a shaped or circular cutter about 8 cm (3 inches) in diameter to cut twelve biscuits, then lay on the prepared baking trays and chill for 20 minutes. Preheat the oven to moderate 180°C (350°F/Gas 4). Bake the biscuits for 20–25 minutes, or until light golden, then cool completely on a wire rack.

4 To make the mascarpone cream, beat together all the ingredients with a wooden spoon until smooth. Spoon neatly onto half the ginger shortbreads, arrange three apricot halves over the cream and top with the remaining shortbreads, pressing gently to secure. Dust with the icing sugar. To serve, place onto serving plates and drizzle a little reserved syrup around the desserts.

Chef's tips The shortbreads, apricots and mascarpone cream can all be prepared up to 2 days in advance. Store the biscuits in an airtight container and refrigerate the fruit and cream, bringing the apricots back to room temperature before assembling the dessert.

If you have any remaining dough, it can be made into ginger biscuits.

Danish pastries

Although this recipe may be time consuming, nothing quite matches the taste of freshly made, rich and flaky yeast dough. The chocolate-rum filling inside the rings is decadence itself.

Preparation time **3 hours + 1 hour 10 minutes chilling + 30 minutes proving**
Total cooking time **40 minutes**
Makes 28

1 kg (2 lb) strong or plain flour
90 g (3 oz) caster sugar
1 tablespoon salt
700 ml (23¼ fl oz) milk
30 g (1 oz) fresh yeast or 15 g (½ oz) dried yeast
450 g (14¼ oz) unsalted butter, chilled
1 egg, beaten
2 egg yolks, beaten to glaze

CHOCOLATE FILLING
125 g (4 oz) marzipan
90 g (3 oz) dark chocolate
2 tablespoons rum

1 Butter and flour two baking trays. Sift the flour, sugar and salt into a large bowl and make a well in the centre. Heat the milk to warm, stir in the yeast and 1 tablespoon of the flour until dissolved, then leave to stand until bubbles form. Add to the dry ingredients and draw in the flour with your fingers until the mixture forms a soft dough. Knead the dough on a floured surface until it is smooth and elastic. Cover with plastic wrap in a bowl and chill for 10 minutes.

2 To make the chocolate filling, bring a pan half-full of water to the boil, then remove from the heat. Have ready a heatproof bowl that will fit over the pan without actually touching the water. Put the marzipan, chocolate and rum in the bowl and place over the pan of steaming water. Stir until melted, then set aside at room temperature to cool and set.

3 On a floured surface, roll out the dough into a rectangle three times as long as it is wide and 3 mm (¹/8 inch) thick. Tap and roll out the butter within two long sheets of plastic wrap into a rectangle, the same width as, but two thirds the length of, the dough. Unwrap and lay the butter on the top two thirds of the dough. Fold the exposed third of the dough up over the butter and fold the top third down.

4 Turn the dough to look like a book, with the binding on the left, and roll again into a rectangle and fold into three. Repeat twice, wrapping in plastic wrap and chilling for 20 minutes between each roll.

5 On a floured surface, roll the dough into a rectangle 3 mm (¹/8 inch) thick. Spread with half the chocolate filling, heating slightly if necessary until it becomes a spreadable consistency. Cut the dough into 1 cm (¹/2 inch) strips across the shorter side and twist each strip to make a spiral. Curl this round to make round pastries in a coiled-rope effect and place on the baking trays.

6 Preheat the oven to hot 220°C (425°F/Gas 7). Set the pastries aside in a warm place to prove for 30 minutes, or until doubled in size. Brush with the beaten egg yolk, being careful to avoid spilling any on the tray, and bake for 15–20 minutes, or until golden. Reglaze the chocolate areas with the remaining filling. Cool on wire racks and serve as soon as possible.

Caramel nut tartlets

Comfort food turns elegant with these rich almond, pecan and brazil nut filled tarts. Serve with creamy sharp Greek yoghurt or crème fraîche.

*Preparation time **25 minutes + 1 hour 20 minutes chilling + cooling***
*Total cooking time **50 minutes***
*Makes **6***

1 quantity shortcrust pastry (see page 58)

CARAMEL NUT FILLING
150 g (5 oz) mixed almonds, pecans and brazil nuts, roughly chopped
250 g (8 oz) caster sugar
1 vanilla pod, split lengthways
125 ml (4 fl oz) thick (double) cream

1 Brush six 8 x 2 cm (3 x 3/4 inch) loose-bottomed tartlet tins with melted butter.
2 Preheat the oven to moderately hot 190°C (375°F/ Gas 5). Roll out the pastry on a floured surface to a 2 mm (1/8 inch) thickness. Cut six 11 cm (41/2 inch) circles to fit the tins, then ease them into the tins, prick the bases with a fork and chill for 20 minutes. Cut six circles of baking paper slightly larger than the tartlet tins and place into the pastry cases. Fill with baking beans or rice. Bake for about 10 minutes. Remove the baking beans or rice and paper from the pastry cases and return to the oven for a further 10 minutes. Cool in the tins on a wire rack.

3 To make the caramel nut filling, place the nuts on a baking tray and toast in a moderate 180°C (350°F/Gas 4) oven for 5–10 minutes, taking care not to let the nuts burn. Place the sugar and vanilla pod into a medium pan with 90 ml (3 fl oz) water and heat gently until dissolved. Raise the heat and cook the sugar for about 10 minutes, or until it becomes a golden caramel. Stir in the cream, standing back a little as it will spit in the caramel. Simmer for 1–2 minutes, then remove from the heat and pass through a fine metal strainer into a bowl. Stir the toasted nuts into the caramel and set aside to cool to room temperature.

4 Spoon the cooled caramel nut filling into the pastry cases and chill for about 1 hour. Remove the tartlets from the tins and serve with some Greek yoghurt or crème fraîche.

Caramel éclairs

With a sophisticated praline filling and crunchy caramel glaze, these éclairs make a lovely change from the more usual chocolate variety.

Preparation time **30 minutes + setting**
Total cooking time **40 minutes**
Makes 12

CHOUX PASTRY
100 g (3¹/4 oz) plain flour
75 g (2¹/2 oz) unsalted butter, cubed
pinch of salt
3 teaspoons caster sugar
3 eggs

1 egg, beaten
60 g (2 oz) flaked almonds
315 g (10 oz) caster sugar
315 ml (10 fl oz) thick (double) cream
45 g (1¹/2 oz) icing sugar, sieved

1 To make the choux pastry, sift the flour onto a sheet of greaseproof paper. Place 125 ml (4 fl oz) water, the butter, salt and sugar in a pan and heat until the butter and water come to the boil. Remove from the heat, add the flour all at once and mix well using a wooden spoon. Return to the heat and beat until a smooth ball forms that leaves the sides of the pan.

2 Remove from the heat and place the pastry in a bowl. Lightly beat the eggs in a small bowl. Using a wooden spoon or electric beaters, add the eggs to the pastry a little at a time, beating well after each addition, until the mixture is smooth and glossy.

3 Preheat the oven to moderate 180°C (350°F/Gas 4).

Thickly butter two baking trays. Place the choux pastry into a piping bag fitted with a large plain tube and pipe twelve even lines of pastry about 13 cm (5 inches) long onto the prepared trays. Brush the éclairs with the beaten egg, taking care not to let any drip onto the trays as this can prevent even rising. Bake for 20–25 minutes, or until crisp, hollow and golden. Immediately remove from the trays and cool on a wire rack.

4 Toast the flaked almonds by placing on a baking tray in the oven for 3–5 minutes, taking care not to burn.

5 Prepare a caramel using the sugar and 90 ml (3 fl oz) water, following the method in the Chef's techniques on page 63.

6 After the caramel has stopped cooking, remelt over a low heat if set and, being very careful not to touch the hot caramel with your fingers, or using tongs to hold the éclairs, dip the top of each éclair into the caramel and leave to set on a wire rack with the caramel uppermost. Lightly oil a baking tray and set aside. Gently reheat the remaining caramel in the pan until melted again, stir in the toasted almonds and pour onto the baking tray, spreading out to form an even layer. Leave to set at room temperature.

7 Whisk the cream with the icing sugar until standing in stiff peaks. Crush the cooled caramel and nuts with a rolling pin or in a food processor until it resembles fine crumbs, then fold into the cream using a large metal spoon or plastic spatula. Place into a piping bag fitted with a medium plain tube and make a small hole in the base of each éclair. Pipe in the filling and serve the éclairs in paper cases as soon as possible.

Citrus millefeuille

With the fresh flavours of orange and lime rind and lemon curd, this pastry is an impressive centrepiece for a special occasion and is completed with a jewel-like kumquat garnish.

*Preparation time **1 hour + 15 minutes chilling***
*Total cooking time **1 hour***
Serves 8

1 quantity puff pastry (see pages 60–61)

PASTRY CREAM
750 ml (24 fl oz) milk
grated rind of 2 limes
9 egg yolks
185 g (6 oz) caster sugar
75 g (2¹/2 oz) plain flour
50 g (1³/4 oz) cornflour

200 g (6¹/2 oz) caster sugar
125 g (4 oz) kumquats, halved
15 g (¹/2 oz) pistachio nuts, skinned
105 g (3¹/2 oz) good-quality lemon curd
grated rind of 1 small orange
icing sugar, to decorate

1 Preheat the oven to hot 210°C (415°F/Gas 6–7). Brush a baking tray with melted butter and line with baking paper. Divide the pastry in two and roll each piece into a 5 mm (¹/4 inch) thick square. Place the squares on two prepared trays and prick all over to prevent the pastry from rising too much. Allow the pastry to chill for 15 minutes. Cover one of the pastry squares with a second sheet of baking paper and another baking tray. Bake for 10–15 minutes. Flip the trays over and return to the oven for 10 minutes, or until the pastry is lightly golden all over. Remove the top baking tray and paper and leave the pastry on a wire rack to cool. Repeat with the other square.

2 To make the pastry cream, place the milk and lime rind in a pan and bring slowly to the boil. In a bowl, whisk the egg yolks with the sugar until light in colour. Sift in the flour and cornflour and whisk until well combined. Pour half the boiling milk into the yolk mixture, whisk well and return to the pan with the remaining milk. Bring to the boil, stirring constantly, and boil for 1 minute to completely cook the flour. Remove from the heat and spread the pastry cream on a tray to cool quickly. Cover the surface with baking paper to prevent a skin forming and leave to cool.

3 Gently heat the caster sugar and 200 ml (6¹/2 fl oz) water in a small pan until the sugar dissolves, then poach the kumquats in the syrup for about 8–10 minutes, or until tender to the point of a knife. Lift the kumquats out of the syrup with a slotted spoon, add to the pistachios and mix with a little extra syrup to give the nuts a shiny coating. Set aside to cool.

4 Trim the edges of the puff pastry with a serrated knife and cut each square in two. Save the neatest piece for the top. Whisk the cooled pastry cream with the lemon curd and orange rind until smooth. Pipe or spoon a third of the pastry cream onto a piece of puff pastry, cover with a second piece of pastry and pipe another third of the cream on top. Repeat with the third piece of pastry and remaining cream. Place the last piece of pastry on top and press lightly. Smooth the sides of the millefeuille with a hot palette knife. Dust the top heavily with icing sugar and scorch lattice lines with a hot skewer following the method in the Chef's techniques on page 63. Decorate the centre of the millefeuille with the poached kumquats and pistachios and serve the same day.

Chocolate and pear tart

Spiced poached pears buried within a creamy chocolate filling and set in crisp chocolate pastry make a beautiful dessert. Pears are a great fruit partner for chocolate in desserts and pastries.

Preparation time **50 minutes + 10 minutes cooling**
Total cooking time **1 hour 30 minutes**
Serves 8

POACHED PEARS
4 small ripe pears
juice of 1 lemon
250 g (8 oz) caster sugar
1/2 vanilla pod, split lengthways
1 star anise
1 small cinnamon stick

1 quantity chocolate pastry (see page 62)
cocoa powder, to dust

CHOCOLATE FILLING
110 ml (3³/4 fl oz) thick (double) cream
55 ml (1³/4 fl oz) whole milk
1/2 vanilla pod, split lengthways
125 g (4 oz) dark chocolate, chopped
1 egg

1 To make the poached pears, peel and halve the pears and core with a melon baller or small knife. Toss in the lemon juice, then remove and set aside. Place the sugar, vanilla pod, star anise, cinnamon and 500 ml (16 fl oz) water into a small pan and heat gently until the sugar has dissolved. Simmer for 5 minutes, then add the pear halves and poach for about 25 minutes, or until tender. Remove the pears and drain on a wire rack over a tray.
2 Brush a loose-bottomed 23 x 3 cm (9 x 1¹/4 inch)

tart tin with melted butter. Roll out the pastry on a lightly floured surface to a 3 mm (¹/8 inch) thickness. Ease the pastry into the prepared tin, then trim the edges neatly. Place the pastry case in the refrigerator and preheat the oven to moderately hot 190°C (375°F/ Gas 5).
3 To make the chocolate filling, heat the cream, milk and vanilla pod in a large pan until almost boiling, then remove from the heat. Add the chocolate and stir until the mixture is perfectly smooth. Allow to cool for about 10 minutes before adding the egg, whisking with a balloon whisk until glossy. Remove the vanilla pod and refrigerate the filling until needed.
4 Cut a circle of baking paper slightly larger than the tin and place into the pastry case. Fill with baking beans or rice. Bake for about 10 minutes. Remove the baking beans or rice and paper from the pastry case and return to the oven for a further 5–10 minutes. Cool in the tin and reduce the oven temperature to warm 160°C (315°F/Gas 2–3).
5 Take the drained pear halves and slice crossways. Arrange in the cooled pastry case with the thinner ends pointing into the centre of the tart. Pour the chocolate filling over the pears to within 3 mm (¹/8 inch) of the top of the pastry case and bake for 30 minutes, or until set around the outside and very slightly wobbly in the centre. Remove from the oven and serve warm or chilled, with a light dusting of cocoa powder and some whipped cream.

Chef's tip If time is short, use tinned pears in place of fresh poached ones and drain very well.

Coffee amaretti mousses

A beautiful, make-ahead dessert for special occasions. These individual coffee liqueur mousses hide a layer of amaretti biscuit and are set on a light sponge base.

Preparation time **1 hour 10 minutes +**
  4 hours chilling
Total cooking time **20 minutes**
Makes 8

SPONGE
2 eggs
60 g (2 oz) caster sugar
30 g (1 oz) plain flour
25 g (³/4 oz) cocoa powder

COFFEE MOUSSE
105 g (3¹/2 oz) caster sugar
3 eggs, separated
1 tablespoon instant coffee dissolved in 1 tablespoon
  water or 2 teaspoons camp coffee
15 g (¹/2 oz) gelatine powder
3 tablespoons coffee liqueur, such as Tia Maria
250 ml (8 fl oz) cream, for whipping

20 amaretti biscuits
150 ml (5 fl oz) thick (double) cream, to decorate
8 chocolate-covered coffee beans, to decorate

1 Line a 22 x 32 cm (8¹/2 x 13 inch) swiss roll tin with baking paper and preheat the oven to moderately hot 190°C (375°F/Gas 5).
2 To make the sponge, whisk the eggs and sugar with electric beaters until thick, pale and tripled in volume. Sieve the flour and cocoa powder twice and fold into the eggs with a large metal spoon. Spread gently over the prepared tin and bake for 5–7 minutes, or until firm to the touch. Turn out onto a wire rack and remove the paper when cool. Cut out eight circles to fit inside eight 8 x 4 cm (3 x 1¹/2 inch) baking rings. Any remaining

sponge can be used for another dessert.
3 To make the coffee mousse, heat the sugar with 4 tablespoons water in a small pan until dissolved, then raise the heat and boil for exactly 2 minutes to make a clear sugar syrup. Make the base for a mousse following the method in the Chef's techniques on page 63, then fold the coffee into the yolk mixture.
4 Meanwhile, place the gelatine in a small pan with the coffee liqueur and leave to stand until spongy. Place on the stove and heat very gently, stirring continuously, for 1–2 minutes, or until the gelatine has completely dissolved. Remove from the heat and cool to room temperature. Whip the cream and, using a large metal spoon, fold into the egg white mixture with the gelatine mixture and yolk mixture, using a figure-of-eight action, until fully combined.
5 Line a baking tray with baking paper, place the baking rings on the tray and put a circle of sponge in the base of each one. Use a ladle to half fill with the coffee mousse. Place a whole amaretti biscuit in the centre, then fill to the rim of the ring with more mousse. Chill for at least four hours, or overnight.
6 An hour before you wish to serve the mousses, hold a hot cloth momentarily around them to help slide off the rings. Crush the remaining amaretti biscuits and press lightly up the sides of the mousses. Whip the cream and put into a piping bag fitted with a small star nozzle. Pipe a rosette of cream onto the middle of each mousse and decorate with the chocolate-covered coffee beans. Chill until ready to serve, then transfer carefully to serving plates using a palette knife.

Chef's tip Small tin cans with the top and bottom removed make a good substitute for the baking rings. Wash thoroughly and line with a strip of baking paper before use.

Choc-in-a-box

Inside each chocolate cube is a layer of chocolate sponge and seasonal red fruit holding up a chocolate lid. These desserts look very impressive but are not as difficult to make as they might seem.

*Preparation time **1 hour 30 minutes***
*Total cooking time **50 minutes***
*Makes **9***

165 g (5¹/2 oz) dark chocolate
150 g (5 oz) unsalted butter, softened
30 g (1 oz) cocoa powder
6 eggs, separated
200 g (6¹/2 oz) caster sugar
90 g (3 oz) plain flour
400 g (12³/4 oz) dark cooking chocolate, finely chopped
150 g (5 oz) apricot jam
250 g (8 oz) redcurrants, raspberries or strawberries
extra cocoa powder, to dust
icing sugar, to dust

1 Line a square 20 x 5 cm (8 x 2 inch) cake tin with foil. Preheat the oven to moderate 180°C (350°F/Gas 4).
2 Bring a pan half-full of water to the boil, then remove from the heat. Have ready a heatproof bowl that will fit over the pan without actually touching the water. Put the dark chocolate, butter and cocoa in the bowl and place over the pan of steaming water. Stir occasionally until the chocolate has melted.
3 Whisk together the egg yolks and sugar until pale in colour, thick, and three times the original volume. Using a balloon whisk, gently stir the chocolate and egg mixtures together. Sieve the flour and fold in gently. In another bowl, whisk the egg whites until soft peaks form, then fold into the chocolate mixture.
4 Pour the mixture into the prepared tin, levelling the surface, and bake for 35–40 minutes. Cool in the tin for 5 minutes before turning out onto a wire rack and removing the foil. When completely cool, use a serrated knife to trim off the sides and level the top.
5 Melt the cooking chocolate in a bowl over a pan of steaming water as before. Place a large sheet of crinkle-free foil on a work surface and spread the chocolate over it, smoothing with a palette knife to a 3 mm (¹/8 inch) thickness. You can do this in two batches if you prefer. Leave to set at room temperature.
6 Once set, mark the chocolate with a ruler into thirty-six 4.5 x 6 cm (1³/4 x 2¹/2 inch) rectangles, and nine 6 cm (2¹/2 inch) square lids and cut with a sharp knife. Set aside layered with baking paper. Cut the cake into nine equal squares.
7 In a small pan, gently heat the apricot jam and brush over the sides of the cake squares. Press a rectangle of chocolate against each side, fill the box up with the fruit and prop up the squares on top. Dust with cocoa and icing sugar and serve with crème fraîche.

Cherry brandy snap baskets

You can make the brandy snap baskets and the ice cream for this pretty and unusual dessert in advance, then just fill the baskets when you're ready to serve.

*Preparation time **20 minutes + 30 minutes chilling***
*Total cooking time **15 minutes***
Makes 6

BRANDY SNAP BASKETS
60 g (2 oz) unsalted butter
60 g (2 oz) light brown sugar
2 tablespoons golden syrup
60 g (2 oz) plain flour
few drops of vanilla extract or essence

500 ml (16 fl oz) vanilla ice cream, preferably
* home-made*
425 g (13¹/2 oz) morello cherries, stoned, drained and
* finely chopped*
2 tablespoons port
sprigs of fresh mint, to decorate

1 To make the brandy snap baskets, place the butter, sugar and golden syrup in a small pan and heat gently until the sugar has dissolved. Cool for 1 minute, then stir in the flour and vanilla extract. Transfer to a small bowl and chill for 30 minutes. Preheat the oven to moderate 180°C (350°F/Gas 4).

2 Remove the ice cream from the freezer and leave to slightly soften for 10 minutes, without allowing to melt. Mix the cherries and port into the softened ice cream. Cover and return to the freezer to firm up.

3 Line two baking trays with baking paper. Divide the brandy snap dough into six even-sized pieces and roll into round balls. Place three on each tray, leaving plenty of space between them, and flatten into a circle with moistened fingertips. Bake for 5–6 minutes.

4 Have ready six teacups upside down on the work surface. Allow the biscuits to rest for 1 minute after baking, then use a palette knife to drape one over each cup, pressing it into a basket shape. Leave until cold and set into shape.

5 Set a basket in the centre of each plate and fill with two scoops of ice cream. Serve immediately, decorated with a sprig of mint.

Financiers

Sour cherries and kirsch give a sweet sharpness to these dainty French almond cakes. Serve whenever you need a sweet treat to go with tea or coffee.

*Preparation time **30 minutes***
*Total cooking time **15 minutes***
Makes 14

60 g (2 oz) dried sour cherries, roughly chopped
60 ml (2 fl oz) kirsch
60 g (2 oz) plain flour
60 g (2 oz) ground almonds
120 g (4 oz) unsalted butter, melted
5 egg whites, lightly beaten
120 g (4 oz) caster sugar

1 Preheat the oven to moderately hot 200°C (400°F/ Gas 6). Place the sour cherries in a small bowl with the kirsch (this can be done up to two hours in advance for a more pronounced flavour). Brush fourteen 40 ml (1¹/4 fl oz) fluted tartlet tins with melted butter and place on a baking tray.
2 Sieve the flour and ground almonds together twice into a medium bowl. Add the melted butter, egg whites and sugar and mix with a wooden spoon or spatula until smooth and well combined. Drain the sour cherries, reserving the kirsch, then add the cherries to the mixture and stir in. Spoon into the prepared tins.
3 Bake for 10–12 minutes, or until golden and risen. Cool on a wire rack. Once cooled, remove from the tins, soak the biscuits in the reserved kirsch and serve with tea or coffee.

Chef's tip This recipe can also be made with sultanas instead of the sour cherries.

Almond lime biscotti

Simple and delicious, these twice-cooked biscuits can be made ahead of time to be served with a sorbet or ice cream.

*Preparation time **20 minutes***
*Total cooking time **1 hour 15 minutes***
Makes 30

5 egg whites
185 g (6 oz) caster sugar
185 g (6 oz) plain flour
grated rind of 3 limes
185 g (6 oz) whole almonds, skin on

1 Preheat the oven to moderate 180°C (350°F/Gas 4) and line a 1 kg (2 lb) loaf tin with baking paper.
2 Whisk the egg whites until standing in soft peaks, then add the sugar and continue to whisk until stiff and glossy. Sieve the flour and fold into the mixture with the lime rind and whole almonds. Spread evenly in the prepared tin, bake for 45 minutes, then cool in the tin.
3 Lower the oven temperature to very slow 100°C (200°F/Gas ¹/4). Remove the mixture from the tin and discard the baking paper. Using a thin sharp knife, slice across the loaf very thinly and lay the biscuits in a single layer on baking trays. Bake at the lower temperature for about 35 minutes, or until the biscuits are very dry, crisp and just golden around the edges. The biscuits can be served with fruit mousses, sorbets, ice cream or a glass of liqueur. Store in an airtight container.

Hazelnut opéra

*Adapted from a complex French recipe, this version uses a hazelnut butter cream
along with the traditional coffee and chocolate flavourings.*

*Preparation time **1 hour 45 minutes + refrigeration***
*Total cooking time **1 hour***
*Serves **6–8***

SPONGE
75 g (2¹/₂ oz) icing sugar
2¹/₂ tablespoons plain flour
75 g (2¹/₂ oz) ground almonds
3 eggs
15 g (¹/₂ oz) unsalted butter, melted and cooled
3 egg whites
1 tablespoon caster sugar

CHOCOLATE GANACHE
150 g (5 oz) dark chocolate, finely chopped
150 ml (5 fl oz) thick (double) cream

COFFEE SYRUP
3 tablespoons caster sugar
3 tablespoons instant coffee

HAZELNUT BUTTER CREAM
70 g (2¹/₄ oz) caster sugar
1 egg white
100 g (3¹/₄ oz) unsalted butter softened
2 tablespoons chocolate hazelnut paste

1 To make the sponge, preheat the oven to hot 220°C (425°F/Gas 7). Line a 22 x 32 cm (9 x 13 inch) swiss roll tray with baking paper. Sift the icing sugar and flour into a large bowl. Stir in the almonds, then add the eggs and whisk until pale. Fold in the butter. Whisk the egg whites until stiff, add the sugar and whisk until stiff peaks form. Whisk a third of the egg white mixture into the almond mixture, then carefully fold in the remaining egg whites until just combined. Pour onto the tray and gently spread. Bake for 6–7 minutes, or until golden and springy. Loosen the edges with the point of a knife and turn out onto a wire rack covered with baking paper. Do not remove the paper used in baking.

2 To make the chocolate ganache, put the chocolate in a bowl. Bring the cream to the boil in a pan and pour onto the chocolate. Stand for a few minutes, then stir until the chocolate is completely melted and smooth.

3 To make the coffee syrup, put the sugar and 185 ml (6 fl oz) water in a pan and stir until dissolved. Bring to the boil, mix in the coffee and remove from the heat.

4 To make the hazelnut butter cream, put the sugar and 3 teaspoons of water into a small heavy-based pan. Stir over low heat until the sugar dissolves completely. Using a wet pastry brush, brush any sugar crystals from the side of the pan. Increase the heat and boil, without stirring, until the sugar reaches the soft-ball stage, which is around 120°C (250°F). If you don't have a sugar thermometer, drop 1/4 teaspoon of the syrup into iced water. The ball of syrup should hold its shape but be soft when pressed.

5 Meanwhile, whisk the egg white until very soft peaks form. Continue whisking and carefully pour in the hot syrup, pouring between the beaters and side of the bowl. Whisk until cold. Gradually whisk in the butter and the chocolate hazelnut paste until well combined.

6 Cut the sponge into three 20 x 10 cm (8 x 4 inch) pieces, discarding the paper. Soak one piece with a third of the coffee syrup, then spread with half the butter cream. Cover with the second piece of sponge, soak with syrup and spread with half the ganache. Cover with the last piece of sponge, soak with the remaining syrup and top with the remaining butter cream. Smooth the top and chill until the butter cream is firmly set.

7 Melt the remaining ganache over a pan of simmering water. Cool until spreadable and spread over the top of the cake. Cut into squares or diamonds.

Fruit tartlets

These traditional pastries are at their best when there is a summer glut of red fruit and berries. You can also make one large tart, which would be the perfect end to a summer picnic.

*Preparation time **45 minutes + 30 minutes chilling***
*Total cooking time **30 minutes***
Makes 6

PASTRY CREAM
315 ml (10 fl oz) milk
90 ml (3 fl oz) lemon juice
grated rind of 2 lemons
4 egg yolks
100 g (3¹/4 oz) caster sugar
2 tablespoons plain flour
2 tablespoons cornflour

1 quantity sweet pastry (see page 59)
400 g (12³/4 oz) mixed berries
100 g (3¹/4 oz) apricot jam

1 Brush six 8 x 2 cm (3 x ³/4 inch) loose-bottomed tartlet tins with melted butter. Preheat the oven to moderately hot 200°C (400°F/Gas 6).

2 To make the pastry cream, place the milk, lemon juice and rind in a pan and bring slowly to the boil. In a bowl, whisk the egg yolks with the sugar until light in colour. Sift in the flour and cornflour and whisk until well combined. Pour half the boiling milk into the yolk mixture, whisk well and return to the pan with the remaining milk. Bring to the boil, stirring constantly, and boil for 1 minute to completely cook the flour. Remove from the heat and spread the pastry cream onto a tray to cool quickly. Cover the surface with baking paper to prevent a skin forming and leave to cool. When cool, whisk until smooth.

3 Roll out the pastry on a floured surface to a 3 mm (¹/8 inch) thickness. Cut six 12 cm (5 inch) circles of pastry to fit the tins, then ease into the tins, prick the bases with a fork and chill for 20 minutes. Cut six circles of baking paper slightly larger than the tartlet tins and place into the pastry cases. Fill with baking beans or rice. Bake for about 10 minutes. Remove the baking beans or rice and paper from the pastry cases and return to the oven for a further 5 minutes, or until golden. Remove the fruit tartlets from the oven, rest for 2 minutes, then remove from their tins and place on a wire rack to cool.

4 Pipe or spoon the pastry cream into the pastry cases to three quarters-full, levelling the surface, then pile the berries on top so that the tarts look generously filled.

5 In a small pan, heat the apricot jam with 3 tablespoons water. When the mixture begins to boil, sieve into a bowl and, while still hot, brush a thin layer of glaze over the cooled tartlets. Serve warm or at room temperature.

Individual lemon cheesecakes

Refreshingly lemony with a gingernut base, the ever-popular cheesecake is here served in individual portions with a red grape jelly top.

Preparation time **20 minutes + 1 hour chilling + overnight chilling**
Total cooking time **5 minutes**
Makes **6**

155 g (5 oz) gingernut biscuits
60 g (2 oz) unsalted butter, melted
300 g (10 oz) full-fat cream cheese
grated rind and juice of 3 lemons
375 g (12 oz) condensed milk
155 g (5 oz) natural or Greek-style yoghurt
2 level teaspoons gelatine powder
185 ml (6 fl oz) red grape juice

1 Place the biscuits in a plastic bag and crush them using a rolling pin, then stir in the melted butter. Alternatively, place in a food processor and use the pulse button to produce fine crumbs. Drizzle over the melted butter and pulse again until thoroughly mixed into the crumbs.
2 Set six 8 x 7 cm (3 x 2³/4 inch) baking rings (see Chef's tips) onto a small tray lined with baking paper and divide the crumb mixture between them. Press the crumbs into the base of the rings using a flat-bottomed glass. Chill while you make the filling.

3 In a medium bowl using electric beaters or in the clean food processor, combine the cream cheese, lemon rind and juice and condensed milk until completely smooth. Add the yoghurt and blend for a few seconds just to combine. Divide the cheese mixture between the rings, leaving a small gap at the top for the jelly, then place in the refrigerator overnight to set.
4 In a small pan, sprinkle the gelatine over half the grape juice and leave to stand until spongy. Place over a low heat and whisk until the gelatine has completely dissolved. Remove from the heat, stir in the remaining grape juice and cool to room temperature. Carefully spoon a layer of grape jelly over each cheesecake, then chill in the refrigerator for 1 hour.
5 To serve, hold a hot cloth momentarily around the cheesecakes to help slide off the rings, then transfer carefully to serving plates using a palette knife.

Chef's tips Small tin cans with the top and bottom removed make a good substitute for the ring moulds. Wash thoroughly and line with a strip of baking paper before use.

If your baking rings are not tall enough, line them with a collar of baking paper to give added height.

Marron barquettes

A barquette is a small, delicate boat-shaped tartlet, here filled with a chestnut (marron in French) cream that has been mixed with a little rum.

*Preparation time **50 minutes + 40 minutes chilling***
*Total cooking time **15 minutes***
*Makes **12***

CHESTNUT CREAM
250 g (8 oz) tinned chestnut purée
2 tablespoons rum
250 ml (8 fl oz) cream, for whipping

1 quantity chocolate pastry (see page 62)
2 whole marrons glacés, to decorate

1 To make the chestnut cream, place the chestnut purée and rum in a large bowl and lightly whisk with a balloon whisk until loosened. Whip the cream until soft peaks form and fold four-fifths of it into the chestnut mixture. The mixture should be standing in firm peaks. Cover and place in the refrigerator for 20 minutes. Whip the remaining cream until stiff and put into a piping bag fitted with a small star nozzle. Place in the refrigerator to chill as well.

2 Preheat the oven to moderately hot 190°C (375°F/ Gas 5). Lightly brush twelve 8 cm (3 inch) long barquette moulds with oil. Roll out the chocolate pastry on a lightly floured surface to a 3 mm (1/8 inch) thickness. Cut into twelve rectangles slightly larger than the moulds, then ease them into the tins. Trim the edges neatly, prick the bases with a fork and chill for 20 minutes. Cut twelve pieces of baking paper slightly larger than the barquette moulds and place into the pastry cases. Fill with baking beans or rice. Bake for about 10–15 minutes, or until dry and firm. Cool completely on a wire rack and remove the baking beans or rice and paper from the pastry case.

3 Using a small spoon, fill each mould with the chestnut cream and shape into a raised peak using a small round-bladed knife that has been put under hot running water and dried. Using the reserved cream, pipe a thin, neat scalloped line of cream on the ridge of each barquette. Cut each marron glacé into six pieces with a small sharp knife and place a piece on the top of each barquette. Serve immediately or chill the barquettes for up to two hours.

Orange bavarois dome

A spectacular bright dome of orange slices clothes a creamy orange mousse centre and liqueur-soaked sponge for a very special dessert.

*Preparation time **1 hour + 30 minutes freezing +
4 hours chilling***
*Total cooking time **25 minutes***
Serves 8

2 whole oranges
250 g (8 oz) caster sugar
2 tablespoons orange liqueur, such as Cointreau

SPONGE
2 eggs
60 g (2 oz) caster sugar
60 g (2 oz) plain flour

ORANGE MOUSSE
105 g (3¹/2 oz) caster sugar
3 eggs, separated
15 g (¹/2 oz) gelatine powder
juice of 1 orange
2 tablespoons orange liqueur, such as Cointreau
250 ml (8 fl oz) cream, for whipping
grated rind of 2 oranges

1 Place the two oranges in the freezer for 30 minutes. Line a swiss roll tin with baking paper and preheat the oven to moderately hot 190°C (375°F/Gas 5).

2 To make the sponge, whisk the eggs and sugar with electric beaters until thick, pale, and tripled in volume. Sieve the flour twice and fold into the eggs with a large metal spoon. Spread gently over the prepared tin and bake for 6–8 minutes, or until firm to the touch. Turn out onto a wire rack and remove the paper when cool.

3 Place the 250 g (8 oz) caster sugar in a wide pan with 200 ml (6¹/2 fl oz) water and heat gently until the sugar has dissolved. Bring to a simmer and remove the oranges from the freezer. Using a very sharp knife or a mandolin,

and protecting your hands with a cloth, slice the orange into 3 mm (¹/8 inch) slices. Drop into the simmering syrup and poach until the pith and skin are tender, testing the skin with the point of a knife. Remove the slices with a slotted spoon and drain on a wire rack. Reduce the syrup by two thirds, remove from the heat and stir in the orange liqueur. Set aside.

4 To make the orange mousse, heat the sugar with 4 tablespoons water in a small pan until dissolved, then raise the heat and boil for exactly 2 minutes to make a clear sugar syrup. Make a base for the mousse following the method in the Chef's techniques on page 63.

5 Meanwhile, place the gelatine in a small pan with the orange juice and leave to stand until spongy. Place on the stove and heat very gently, stirring continuously, for 1–2 minutes, or until the gelatine has completely dissolved. Remove from the heat, add the liqueur and cool to room temperature. Whip the cream and, using a large metal spoon, fold into the egg white mixture with the gelatine mixture, orange rind and yolk mixture, using a figure-of-eight action, until fully combined.

6 Take a 1.25 litre rounded basin, preferably stainless steel, and turn upside down onto the sponge. Cut around the edge with a sharp knife, remove the basin and trim a little so that the sponge will just fit inside it. Use the orange slices to line the inside of the basin, making sure you have a neat edge around the top. Ladle the orange mousse into the basin, being careful not to disturb the fruit, and top with the sponge disc, pressing it in very gently to remove any trapped air underneath. Brush the sponge generously with some of the reserved orange syrup, cover with plastic wrap and chill for at least four hours or overnight.

7 To serve, hold a hot cloth momentarily around the basin to release the mousse and invert onto a serving plate. Brush gently with a thin layer of the orange syrup and cut into wedges with a sharp serrated knife.

Orange flower crème caramel

*A refreshing and elegant dessert that can be prepared a day before if you wish,
making it an ideal sweet finish to a dinner party.*

*Preparation time **25 minutes + 4 hours chilling***
*Total cooking time **55 minutes***
*Makes **6***

220 g (7 oz) caster sugar
500 ml (16 fl oz) milk
1/2 vanilla pod, split lengthways
grated rind of 1 orange
3 eggs, beaten
2 egg yolks
1 teaspoon orange flower water

1 Preheat the oven to slow 150°C (300°F/Gas 2).
2 Prepare a caramel using 90 g (3 oz) of the sugar and a tablespoon of water, following the method in the Chef's techniques on page 63. After the caramel has stopped cooking, reheat over a low heat if set, then pour into six 125 ml (4 fl oz) ramekins. Tip a little to coat the sides and bottom of the ramekins, holding them in a cloth to protect your hands.
3 Bring the milk, vanilla pod and orange rind to the boil slowly in a small pan. In a bowl, whisk together the eggs, egg yolks, remaining sugar and the orange flower water until creamy, then whisk in the boiling milk and pour through a sieve into a jug, discarding the vanilla pod and rind.
4 Pour the mixture onto the caramel in the ramekins and place them in a roasting tin. Fill the tin with hot water a third of the way up the ramekins and bake for about 30–35 minutes, or until just set. Remove the ramekins from the roasting tin and chill for at least 4 hours or overnight.
5 To serve, run the blade of a palette knife around the edge of each crème caramel, then place the centre of a dessert plate over the ramekin and invert onto the plate, carefully lifting off the ramekin and allowing the liquid caramel to run over the dessert.

Pineapple miroirs

A delicate sponge and mousse assembly found in most patisseries, this version has sweet fresh pineapple showing under the 'mirror' glaze.

Preparation time **35 minutes + 6 hours chilling**
Total cooking time **20 minutes**
Makes 6

SPONGE
2 eggs
60 g (2 oz) caster sugar
60 g (2 oz) plain flour

250 g (8 oz) sugar
**2 ripe baby pineapples, peeled and eyes removed
(see Chef's tips)**
30 g (1 oz) icing sugar
4 level teaspoons gelatine powder
3 tablespoons white rum
155 ml (5 fl oz) thick (double) cream
250 ml (8 fl oz) plain full-fat yoghurt
90 ml (3 fl oz) clear apple juice

1 Line a 22 x 32 cm (9 x 13 inch) swiss roll tin with baking paper and preheat the oven to moderately hot 190°C (375°F/Gas 5).

2 To make the sponge, whisk the eggs and sugar with electric beaters until thick, pale, and tripled in volume. Sieve the flour twice and fold into the eggs with a large metal spoon. Spread gently over the prepared tin and bake for 6–8 minutes, or until firm to the touch. Turn out onto a wire rack to cool.

3 Place the sugar in a wide pan with 200 ml (6¹/2 fl oz) water and heat gently until the sugar is dissolved and the syrup is simmering. Slice the pineapples very thinly and poach in the syrup for about 3–5 minutes, depending on their ripeness. Remove from the syrup with a slotted spoon and drain on paper towels. Set aside six of the thinnest, neatest slices and reserve the syrup. Place the remaining pineapple into a blender or food processor with the icing sugar. Blend for a few seconds until the fruit is in small pieces but not puréed. Strain off any excess juice, leaving the fruit quite dry.

4 Place 3 teaspoons of the gelatine and the rum in a small pan and leave to stand until spongy. Place on the stove and heat very gently, stirring continuously, for 1–2 minutes, or until the gelatine has completely dissolved. Whip the cream, then add the yoghurt and drained pineapple. When the gelatine has cooled, fold in to the cream.

5 Remove the paper from the sponge and cut six circles to fit the bases of six 8 x 5 cm (3 x 2 inch) baking rings (see Chef's tips). Place a circle in the base of each ring and brush with the reserved syrup. Spoon the pineapple cream into the rings and chill for 4 hours or overnight until firm.

6 Sprinkle the remaining gelatine on the apple juice in a small pan and leave to stand until spongy. Place the pan on the stove and heat very gently, stirring continuously, for 1–2 minutes, or until the gelatine has completely dissolved. Allow to cool while you place a slice of the reserved pineapple on top of each set miroir. Pour over enough apple juice to just barely cover and refrigerate to set the glaze for 1–2 hours. To serve, hold a hot cloth momentarily around each ring to release the miroir onto a serving plate.

Chef's tips You can also use a whole tinned pineapple.

Small tin cans with the top and bottom removed make a good substitute for the baking rings. Wash thoroughly and line with a strips of baking paper before use.

Palmiers

These supremely simple biscuits show off perfect home-made puff pastry to its best effect.

Preparation time **20 minutes**
Total cooking time **20 minutes**
Makes 15

60 g (2 oz) sugar
2 level teaspoons ground cinnamon

1/2 quantity puff pastry (see pages 60–61)

1 Preheat the oven to hot 220°C (425°F/Gas 7) and brush a baking tray with melted butter.
2 Mix the sugar and cinnamon together in a bowl and use instead of flour to dust the work surface. Quickly roll the dough out to a 5 mm (1/4 inch) thick rectangle and sprinkle generously with the sugar and cinnamon. Fold the short sides in three times to meet in the centre, sprinkle with more sugar and cinnamon, then fold in half as if you were closing a book. Cut horizontally across the pastry into 1 cm (1/2 inch) slices and place onto the prepared tray with a cut side uppermost. Flatten gently with a rolling pin and sprinkle with more sugar. Bake for 10 minutes, then turn the palmiers over and bake for a further 10 minutes, or until richly caramelized. Cool on a wire rack.

Chef's tip For a quick dessert, sandwich the palmiers together with 280 ml (9 fl oz) cream whipped together with 1 tablespoon icing sugar and 1 tablespoon brandy.

Almond and hazelnut macaroons

These nutty macaroons are crisp on the outside with a meltingly soft inside.

Preparation time **20 minutes**
Total cooking time **25 minutes**
Makes 36

30 g (1 oz) hazelnuts
30 g (1 oz) ground almonds
125 g (4 oz) icing sugar
2 egg whites
pinch of caster sugar

1 Preheat the oven to moderate 180°C (350°F/Gas 4).
2 Place two baking trays together and line the top tray with baking paper (this will prevent the bottom of the macaroons overbrowning during baking).
3 Toast the hazelnuts by placing on a baking tray and toasting for 3–5 minutes, taking care not to let the hazelnuts burn. Leave to cool, then place in a food processor and pulse until finely ground.
4 Reduce the oven temperature to warm 160°C (315°F/Gas 2–3). Sift the almonds, hazelnuts and icing sugar into a bowl, then sift again to make sure that they are thoroughly mixed. In a separate bowl, whisk the egg whites with the pinch of sugar until stiff and shiny and the mixture forms stiff peaks when the whisk is lifted.
5 Using a metal spoon, carefully fold the dry ingredients into the egg whites, trying not to lose any air. The mixture should be shiny and soft, not liquid.
6 Spoon into a piping bag with a 7.5 mm (1/3 inch) nozzle. Pipe 2 cm (3/4 inch) wide rounds onto the prepared trays, leaving room for expansion. Bake, in two batches if necessary, for 15–20 minutes, or until golden and crisp, checking the macaroons frequently. Cool on the tray for a few minutes, then remove to a wire rack.

Palmiers (left) and Almond and hazelnut macaroons

Lemon meringue tartlets

Lemon meringue pie turns miniature in these little mouthwateringly citrus tarts, each one topped with a light cloud of meringue.

*Preparation time **20 minutes + 20 minutes chilling***
*Total cooking time **35 minutes***
Makes 22

1 quantity shortcrust pastry (see page 58)
4 egg whites
200 g (6¹/₂ oz) caster sugar
2 tablespoons icing sugar

LEMON FILLING
6 egg yolks
250 g (8 oz) caster sugar
4 teaspoons finely grated lemon rind
juice of 4 lemons
60 g (2 oz) unsalted butter

1 Brush two 12-hole (30 ml/1 fl oz capacity) muffin tins with melted butter. Preheat the oven to moderate 180°C (350°F/Gas 4).
2 Roll out the pastry on a floured surface to a 3 mm (¹/₈ inch) thickness. Cut 22 circles of pastry to fit the tins, then ease them into the tins and chill for 20 minutes. Cut 22 circles of baking paper slightly larger than the pastry cases and place in the cases. Fill with baking beans or rice. Bake for about 10 minutes. Remove the baking beans or rice and paper from the cases and return to the oven for a further 5 minutes, or until golden. Remove from the oven, leave to rest for 2 minutes, then cool in their tins on a wire rack.
3 To make the lemon filling, half-fill a pan with water and heat until simmering. Using electric beaters, whisk the egg yolks and sugar in a heatproof bowl that will fit over the pan without actually touching the water, until light and creamy. Add the lemon rind, juice and butter and sit the bowl over the pan of simmering water. Whisk continuously for 10–15 minutes, or until the mixture is thick and creamy and leaves a ribbon as it falls from the whisk. While the filling is still hot, pour into the cases.
4 Preheat the grill to medium. Place the egg whites in a clean dry bowl and beat them with a balloon whisk or electric beaters until soft peaks form. Gradually add the sugar, beating well between each addition, until stiff glossy peaks form. Spoon or pipe onto the lemon filling in the pastry cases and swirl attractively with the tip of a spoon. Sieve the icing sugar over the surface of the tarts and grill for 1–2 minutes, or until the meringue is just tinged golden, then serve as soon as possible.

Plum and apricot tarts

These beautiful fruit tarts combine plums and apricots with a hazelnut cream.
They are delicious served while still warm.

Preparation time **25 minutes + 20 minutes chilling**
Total cooking time **45 minutes**
Makes 6

HAZELNUT CREAM
75 g (2¹/2 oz) unsalted butter, softened
75 g (2¹/2 oz) caster sugar
I egg, lightly beaten
110 g (3³/4 oz) finely ground hazelnuts or almond meal
1¹/2 tablespoons plain flour
3 teaspoons rum

I quantity sweet pastry (with I teaspoon cinnamon
  added to the flour) (see page 59)
180 g (5³/4 oz) ripe plums, halved and stoned
180 g (5³/4 oz) ripe apricots, halved and stoned
50 g (1³/4 oz) apricot jam

1 Brush six 8 x 2 cm (3 x ³/4 inch) fluted loose-bottomed tartlet tins with melted butter.
2 To make the hazelnut cream, beat the butter and sugar together using a wooden spoon or electric beaters until light and creamy. Gradually add the egg, a third at a time, beating well between each addition. Stir in 80 g (2³/4 oz) of the ground hazelnuts or almond meal, the flour and the rum and set aside.

3 Roll out the pastry on a floured surface to a 3 mm (¹/8 inch) thickness. Cut six 12 cm (5 inch) circles of pastry to fit the tins, then ease into the tins, prick the bases with a fork and chill for 20 minutes. Preheat the oven to moderate 180°C (350°F/Gas 4).
4 Sprinkle the remaining ground hazelnuts or almond meal on the base of the pastry, then spread or pipe the hazelnut cream into the cases. Smooth the surface and top three of the tarts with plum halves and three with apricot halves, cut-side-down. Bake in the oven for 30–40 minutes, or until the hazelnut cream is lightly golden and puffed and the pastry cooked through (you may need to cover the tarts with foil and place close to the bottom of the oven for the final 10 minutes). Cool in the tins, then place on a wire rack.
5 In a small pan, heat the apricot jam with 1 tablespoon water. When the mixture has melted and begins to boil, sieve it into a small bowl and, while still hot, brush a thin layer of glaze over the cooled tartlets and serve warm or at room temperature.

Chef's tip The sprinkling of ground hazelnuts or almond meal in the base of the pastry case helps to soak up the fruit juice from the plums and apricots and keeps the pastry crisp.

Pavlovas with fragrant fruit

These dramatic, feather-light mounds of pillowy meringue are a treat when combined with champagne-steeped fruit and creamy Greek yoghurt.

*Preparation time **20 minutes***
*Total cooking time **2 hours 10 minutes***
Makes 6

PAVLOVAS
6 egg whites
220 g (7 oz) caster sugar
I teaspoon white wine vinegar
2 teaspoons boiling water

60 g (2 oz) caster sugar
***1/2* vanilla pod, split lengthways**
250 ml (8 fl oz) sparkling wine or champagne
I kg (2 lb) mixed soft fruit, such as strawberries,
   raspberries, stoned black cherries and blackberries
280 ml (9 fl oz) thick (double) cream
I 1/2 tablespoons icing sugar
185 ml (6 fl oz) Greek yoghurt
I 1/2 tablespoons kirsch

1 Preheat the oven to very slow 120°C (250°F/ Gas 1/2). Line two large baking trays with baking paper.
2 To make the pavlovas, place the egg whites in a clean dry bowl and beat them with a balloon whisk or electric beaters until soft peaks form. Gradually add the sugar, vinegar and boiling water and whisk continuously until the meringue is thick and glossy. Using two large wet metal spoons, divide and shape the meringue into six ovals and place on the prepared baking trays. Cook for about 1 1/2–2 hours, or until the pavlovas are pale and crisp on the outside with soft, chewy centres.

3 To prepare the fruit, place the sugar in a large pan with the vanilla pod and sparkling wine and heat gently until simmering. Simmer for 5 minutes, then remove from the heat. Add the fruit and set aside to cool, during which time the soft fruit will gently poach in the cooling liquid. Remove the vanilla pod from the fruit just before serving.
4 Using a balloon whisk, whip the cream until it just forms soft peaks, then sift in the icing sugar and fold in with the yoghurt and kirsch.
5 To serve the dessert, place the pavlovas on plates and top with a generous spoon of kirsch-flavoured cream. Place two tablespoons of the fruit on top of each pavlova, allowing the juice to drizzle down the sides, and serve the remaining fruit around the base of the dessert or in a separate bowl.

Chef's tip If you prefer a neater shape for the pavlovas, pipe six rounds using a piping bag with a plain 2 cm (3/4 inch) nozzle.

Croissants

Croissants require time and effort to produce, but the rich buttery results will astound friends and family. Served warm with jam or marmalade, they are guaranteed to disappear at an alarming rate!

Preparation time 3 hours + resting + chilling overnight
Total cooking time 20 minutes
Makes 12–16

500 g (1 lb) plain flour
1 teaspoon salt
50 g (1³/4 oz) caster sugar
320 ml (10 fl oz) milk
15 g (¹/2 oz) fresh yeast or 7 g (¹/4 oz) dried yeast
340 g (10³/4 oz) unsalted butter, at room temperature
2 egg yolks, lightly beaten
whole almonds, to decorate

ALMOND CREAM
60 g (2 oz) unsalted butter, softened
60 g (2 oz) caster sugar
1 egg, beaten
60 g (2 oz) ground almonds
15 g (¹/2 oz) plain flour
rind of ¹/2 lemon

1 Sift the flour, salt and sugar into a large bowl and make a well in the centre. Heat the milk to warm, stir in the yeast and 1 tablespoon of the flour until dissolved, then leave to stand until bubbles form. Add to the dry ingredients and bring together to form a soft dough, then tip out onto a floured work surface and knead for 5 minutes, or until smooth and elastic. Transfer the dough to a floured bowl and cover. Set aside in a warm area for about 1 hour, or until doubled in volume.

2 Meanwhile, put the butter between two sheets of plastic wrap and roll into a rectangle measuring about 20 x 10 cm (8 x 4 inches).

3 Once the dough has risen, punch it down and transfer to a floured work surface. Roll into a rectangle about 40 x 12 cm (16 x 5 inches). The dough should be just over twice as long as the butter and a little bit wider. Place the butter on the lower half of the dough and fold the dough over to completely enclose the butter. Seal the edges with your fingertips. Turn the dough so that the fold is on the right-hand side and lightly roll the dough into a large rectangle twice as long as it is wide. Brush off excess flour and fold the dough into even thirds like a letter, with the bottom third up and the top third down. Chill in plastic wrap for 20 minutes.

4 To make the almond cream, beat the butter and sugar together using a wooden spoon or electric beaters, until light and creamy. Gradually add the egg, a third at a time, beating well between each addition. Stir in the ground almonds, flour and lemon rind.

5 Remove the dough from the refrigerator and cut it in half. On a well-floured surface, roll each piece of dough into a large rectangle, and trim it to 22 x 36 cm (8³/4 x 4¹/2 inches). Using a triangular template with a base of 18 cm (7 inches) and sides of 14 cm (5¹/2 inches), cut the rectangles into six triangles (you should be left with two end triangles). Along the wide end of the triangle, pull down to form a longer triangle and spoon a little almond cream onto the wide base. Roll the dough up, starting from the wide end, to form crescents, tucking the triangular point underneath the dough. Place the croissants on baking trays and lightly brush with the egg yolk. Cover with plastic wrap and refrigerate overnight.

6 Remove the croissants from the refrigerator and set aside to rise for 30–45 minutes, or until double in size. Do not hurry this process by putting the croissants anywhere too warm, or the butter in the dough will melt. Preheat the oven to moderately hot 200°C (400°F/Gas 6). Toast the almonds under a medium grill until golden.

7 Once the croissants have doubled in size, gently brush with a second layer of egg and decorate with the almonds. Bake for 15–20 minutes, or until golden.

Passion fruit tart

*This tart has a gloriously golden filling, for which you'll need about nine ripe passion fruit. At the end,
it is placed quickly under the grill to give it a caramelized top.*

Preparation time **25 minutes + 2 hours
30 minutes chilling**
Total cooking time **1 hour 15 minutes**
Serves 8

1 quantity sweet pastry (see page 59)
icing sugar, for caramelizing

PASSION FRUIT FILLING
150 ml (5 fl oz) thick (double) cream
100 g (3¼ oz) caster sugar
**200 ml (6½ fl oz) passion fruit pulp (including seeds),
about 9 fruit**
4 eggs

1 Preheat the oven to moderately hot 190°C (375°F/
Gas 5). Brush a loose-bottomed tart tin, about 20 cm
(8 inches) across and 4 cm (1½ inches) deep with
melted butter.

2 Roll out the pastry on a floured surface to a
3 mm (⅛ inch) thickness. Ease the pastry into the tin,
pressing the pastry into the corners, then trim the edges
neatly. Prick the base lightly with a fork and chill for
30 minutes. Cut a circle of baking paper slightly larger
than the tin and place into the pastry case. Fill with
baking beans or rice. Bake for about 10 minutes.
Remove the baking beans or rice and paper from the
pastry case and return to the oven for a further
5 minutes, or until golden. Place on a wire rack to cool
in the tin. Reduce the oven temperature to very slow
140°C (275°F/Gas 1).

3 To make the passion fruit filling, warm the cream in
a small pan over low heat. In a large bowl, whisk the
sugar and passion fruit pulp with a balloon whisk, then
whisk in the eggs. Stir in the warmed cream and pass the
mixture through a fine sieve into a wide jug, pressing
the passion fruit seeds down with the back of a spoon to
extract as much juice as possible.

4 Place the cooled pastry case onto a baking tray,
carefully pour the passion fruit mixture into the pastry
case from the jug and gently slide the tart into the oven,
being careful not to let any of the filling spill over. Bake
for 50–55 minutes, or until the filling is just firm around
the outside but a little wobbly in the centre.

5 Leave to cool completely, then remove from the tin
and chill for several hours to allow the centre to firm up.
Just before serving, dust the surface of the tart evenly
with the icing sugar and caramelize under a hot grill for
a few seconds to make a thin, golden glaze.

Peach condé

A condé is a dessert made with rice and poached fruit. Here the fruit is peaches, poached in a dessert wine and hidden between layers of creamy rice.

Preparation time **1 hour + overnight chilling**
Total cooking time **1 hour 5 minutes**
Makes 4

POACHED PEACHES
375 ml (12 fl oz) dessert wine
1 vanilla pod, split lengthways
90 g (3 oz) caster sugar
2 ripe peaches

3 tablespoons short-grain rice, rinsed and drained
600 ml (20 fl oz) milk
2 tablespoons caster sugar
3 teaspoons gelatine powder
155 ml (5 fl oz) thick (double) cream
60 g (2 oz) dark chocolate
1 tablespoon seedless red jam

1   To make the poached peaches, place the wine, vanilla pod and sugar into a pan and bring to the boil, then turn down to a simmer and simmer for 5 minutes. Place the peaches in the syrup and poach for 15 minutes, or until tender, turning the peaches once if not completely covered by the syrup. Remove the peaches from the syrup and drain on a wire rack. Continue to simmer the syrup until reduced by half, then remove and reserve the vanilla pod. When the peaches are cool, slip off the skins, remove the stones and dice the flesh.

2   Place the rice, milk and reserved vanilla pod in a medium heavy-based pan and bring slowly to the boil. Simmer, stirring often, for about 30 minutes, or until the rice is soft and creamy. Remove from the heat, remove the vanilla pod and stir in the sugar. Immediately sprinkle the gelatine powder over the rice and leave for 1 minute to dissolve before stirring well. Cool the rice for a few minutes. Using a balloon whisk or electric beaters, whip the cream until it just forms soft peaks, then fold into the cooling rice.

3   Place half the rice into four 200 ml (6½ fl oz) moulds, sprinkle the diced peach on top and cover with the remaining rice. Level the surface of the puddings and chill until set, preferably overnight.

4   Bring a pan half-full of water to the boil, then remove from the heat. Have ready a heatproof bowl that will fit over the pan without actually touching the water. Put the chocolate in the bowl and place over the pan of steaming water. Stir occasionally until the chocolate has melted.

5   Make two small piping bags out of triangles of baking paper. Unmould the set rice puddings by holding a hot cloth momentarily around them to help slide off the moulds and inverting onto serving plates. Fill one of the piping bags with the melted chocolate and snip off the point to make a tiny hole. Pipe a simple flower shape and a row of joined dots on top of each pudding. The chocolate will set quickly on the cold puddings.

6   Beat the red jam with a spoon until softened and place into the second piping bag. Cut a little more off the tip to make a slightly larger hole than before and carefully fill the petals of the flower with jam. The reserved poaching syrup can be poured around the peach condés to serve or used instead as a sauce for ice cream or other desserts.

Praline dacquoise

Dramatically striped and flavoured with light praline butter cream, this dessert can be made up to a day ahead of time and chilled, leaving you precious time when entertaining.

*Preparation time **1 hour 30 minutes +
20 minutes chilling***
*Total cooking time **20 minutes***
Serves 8

ALMOND SPONGE
140 g (4¹/2 oz) ground almonds
65 g (2¹/4 oz) plain flour
230 g (7¹/4 oz) caster sugar
100 ml (3¹/4 fl oz) milk
9 egg whites

HAZELNUT BUTTER CREAM
125 g (4 oz) caster sugar
2 egg whites
155 g (5 oz) unsalted butter, softened
30 g (1 oz) chocolate hazelnut spread

55 g (1³/4 oz) flaked almonds
icing sugar, for decoration
cocoa powder, for decoration

1 Preheat the oven to moderately hot 190°C (375°F/Gas 5). Line a 22 x 32 (8¹/2 x 13 inch) swiss roll tin with baking paper and brush with melted butter.
2 To make the almond sponge, sieve the ground almonds, flour and 170 g (5¹/2 oz) of the caster sugar together into a bowl. Add the milk and 1 egg white and beat with a wooden spoon until smoothly blended. In a separate clean, dry bowl, whisk the remaining egg whites until stiff peaks form, then gradually whisk in the remaining 60 g (2 oz) caster sugar to form a stiff and shiny meringue. Using a large metal spoon or plastic spatula, carefully fold one third of the meringue into the almond sponge mixture until well incorporated, then gently fold in the remaining meringue in three or four

additions. Be careful not to fold too much or the mixture will lose volume.
3 Spread gently over the prepared tray and bake for 7–10 minutes, or until golden and springy. Loosen the edges with the point of a knife and turn out onto a wire rack covered with baking paper. Do not remove the paper used in baking.
4 To make the hazelnut butter cream, put 90 g (3 oz) of the sugar and 60 ml (2 fl oz) water in a small heavy-based pan. Stir over low heat until the sugar dissolves completely. Using a wet pastry brush, brush any sugar crystals from the side of the pan. Increase the heat and boil, without stirring, until the syrup reaches the soft-ball stage, which is around 120°F (250°F). If you don't have a sugar thermometer, drop ¹/4 teaspoon of the syrup into iced water. The ball of syrup should hold its shape but be soft when pressed.
5 Meanwhile, whisk the egg whites until very soft peaks form, then add the remaining sugar and whisk until stiff and glossy. Continue whisking and carefully pour in the hot syrup, pouring between the beaters and the side of the bowl. Whisk until cold. Gradually whisk in the butter and chocolate spread until well combined.
6 Using a serrated knife, trim the edges of the sponge to neaten and cut into three 20 x 10 cm (8 x 4 inch) pieces, discarding the paper. Use one third of the butter cream to cover the first layer of sponge, cover with the second piece and repeat with another third of butter cream. Top with the remaining sponge. Coat the top and sides with the remaining butter cream and smooth with a palette knife. Chill for 20 minutes, or until set.
7 Toast the flaked almonds under a medium grill until golden. Dust the cake with icing sugar. Cut 1 cm (¹/2 inch) strips of paper and lay on top of the cake at 1.5 cm (5/8 inch) intervals. Dust with sifted cocoa and remove the paper carefully to show brown and white lines. Press the toasted almonds onto the sides.

Chef's techniques

◆

Shortcrust pastry

This delicious dough produces one of the most versatile pastries for tarts and flans and is also one of the easiest to make.

*Preparation time **10 minutes + 20 minutes chilling***
*Total cooking time **Nil***
Makes 400 g (12³/₄ oz)

200 g (6¹/₂ oz) plain flour
large pinch of salt
large pinch of caster sugar
100 g (3¹/₄ oz) unsalted butter, chilled
I egg, lightly beaten
I–2 drops vanilla extract or essence

1 In a large bowl, sift together the flour, salt and sugar. Cut the butter into 1 cm (¹/₂ inch) cubes and place in the flour.

2 Rub the butter into the flour using your fingertips until the mixture resembles fine breadcrumbs.

3 Make a well in the centre and pour in the combined egg, 2–3 teaspoons water and the vanilla.

4 Slowly work the mixture together with a palette knife or pastry scraper until it forms a rough ball. If it is slightly sticky, add a little more flour. Turn out onto a lightly floured cool surface, gather the dough into a ball and flatten it slightly. Wrap the pastry in plastic wrap and chill for 20 minutes before using.

Chef's tip This quantity of pastry is sufficient to line two shallow 18–20 cm (7–8 inch) flan tins. If only making one flan or tart, divide the pastry into two and wrap separately in plastic wrap. Use one piece and put the second one in a plastic bag and seal, airtight, to freeze and use on another occasion.

Place the cubes of butter into the flour, salt and sugar and rub into the dry ingredients.

Continue rubbing the butter into the flour until the mixture resembles fine breadcrumbs.

Pour the combined egg, water and vanilla into the well.

Slowly work the mixture together with a palette knife until it forms a rough ball.

Sweet pastry

This pastry is made in a similar way to the shortcrust, but has added sugar for when a tart or flan needs a little extra sweetness.

*Preparation time **10 minutes + 20 minutes chilling***
*Total cooking time **Nil***
Makes 480 g (15¼ oz)

200 g (6½ oz) plain flour
large pinch of salt
70 g (2¼ oz) unsalted butter, chilled
80 g (2¾ oz) caster sugar
I egg, lightly beaten
I–2 drops vanilla extract or essence

1 In a large bowl, sift together the flour and salt. Cut the butter into 1 cm (½ inch) cubes and place in the flour. Rub the butter into the flour using your fingertips until the mixture resembles fine breadcrumbs.

2 Stir in the sugar and make a well in the centre. Pour in the combined egg and vanilla and slowly work the mixture together using a palette knife or pastry scraper. If the dough is too dry, sprinkle it with a little water until it just holds together.

3 Remove the dough from the bowl onto a lightly floured surface. Using the palm of your hand, smear the dough away from you until it is smooth.

4 Gather the dough into a ball and flatten it slightly. Wrap in plastic wrap and place in the refrigerator to chill for 20 minutes before using.

Chef's tip This quantity of pastry is sufficient to line two shallow 18–20 cm (7–8 inch) flan tins. If only making one flan or tart, divide the pastry into two and wrap separately in plastic wrap. Use one piece and put the second one in a plastic bag and seal, airtight, to freeze and use on another occasion.

Sift the flour and salt into a large bowl. Cut the butter into small cubes and rub into the flour.

Stir in the sugar. Make a well in the centre and add the combined egg and vanilla.

Using the palm of your hand, smear the dough away from you on a lightly floured surface until smooth.

Gather the dough into a ball and flatten slightly.

Puff pastry

This pastry requires more effort and time than the other pastries, but the result is a lovely buttery and flaky base for any tart or pastry. If you are short of time, bought blocks or sheets of puff are a good alternative.

Preparation time **1 day**
Total cooking time **Nil**
Makes **530 g (1 lb 1 oz)**

DOUGH BASE
250 g (8 oz) strong or plain flour
1 teaspoon salt
2–3 drops of lemon juice
125 ml (4 fl oz) water
40 g (1 1/4 oz) unsalted butter, melted

100 g (3 1/4 oz) unsalted butter, chilled

1 To make the dough base, sift the flour and salt onto a cool work surface and make a well in the centre. Add the lemon juice to the water, then place in the well with the butter and mix together with your fingertips. With the side of a palette knife or a pastry scraper, use a cutting action to draw in the flour and work it into the butter mixture until the dry flour disappears and the mixture resembles loose crumbs. Draw together with your hands and knead lightly, adding a few drops of water if necessary, to form a smooth soft ball of dough.

2 Cut an 'X' on top of the dough to prevent shrinkage, then wrap in lightly floured greaseproof paper or plastic wrap. Chill for 1 hour in the refrigerator—this will make the dough more pliable for rolling. Place the chilled butter between two pieces of greaseproof paper or plastic wrap. Tap it with the side of a rolling pin and shape into a 2 cm (3/4 inch) thick square. This action will make the butter pliable to roll, without melting it.

3 Unwrap the dough and place it on a lightly floured cool surface. Roll the dough from just off centre to form a cross shape with a mound in the centre.

4 Place the butter on the central mound and fold over the four sides of the dough to enclose it completely.

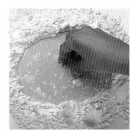

Sift the flour and salt onto a work surface and make a well in the centre. Add the lemon juice, water and butter and blend together with your fingertips.

Cut an 'X' on top of the pastry with a sharp knife.

Unwrap the chilled dough and place it on a lightly floured surface. Roll from just off centre to form a cross shape with a mound in the centre.

Place the butter on the central mound and fold over the four sides of the dough to enclose it.

5 Roll over the top and bottom of the dough to seal the edges. On a lightly floured surface, roll the dough into a 12 x 35 cm (5 x 14 inch) rectangle.

6 Fold in three by folding the bottom third up towards the middle and the top third down. Brush off the excess flour and ensure that the edges all meet neatly. Make an indentation with your finger to record the first roll and fold. Wrap in plastic wrap and chill for 30 minutes.

7 Give the dough a quarter turn with the folded side on your left as if it was a book. With a rolling pin, gently press down to seal the edges.

8 Repeat steps 5–7 three more times, remembering to record each roll with an indentation and chilling for 30 minutes after each roll. After two rolls and folds, you should have two indentations. The finished pastry should have four indentations, and will start to look smoother as you continue to roll and fold. Leave the dough to rest in the refrigerator for a final 30 minutes. The puff pastry is now ready to use. It can be frozen whole, or cut into smaller portions, then used as needed.

Chef's tips When making puff pastry, work on a cool surface to prevent the butter from melting and forming a heavy dough. In hot weather, it may be necessary to refrigerate the dough for an extra 15 minutes during the final resting.

Making puff pastry is not difficult, but it is time consuming, so make two or three quantities at once and freeze the extra. Thaw the pastry by leaving it overnight in the refrigerator. Puff will keep in the refrigerator for 4 days and in the freezer for 3 months.

Seal the edges of the dough by pressing down with a rolling pin. Roll the pastry into a rectangle.

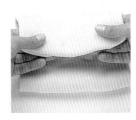

Fold the dough in three by folding the bottom third up towards the middle and the top third down.

After chilling the dough, put it on the surface in front of you as before and turn it a quarter turn so that it looks like a book with the binding on the left. Press down to seal the edges, then roll, fold and chill again.

Continue rolling, folding and chilling, trying to maintain an even finish and neat corners.

Chocolate pastry

The method for this pastry is very similar to that for a plain shortcrust pastry, with some cocoa powder added to give a chocolate flavour and an amazing dark colour.

Preparation time **10 minutes + 20 minutes chilling**
Total cooking time **Nil**
Makes **415 g (13 oz)**

155 g (5 oz) plain flour
large pinch of salt
45 g (1 1/2 oz) cocoa powder
75 g (2 1/2 oz) unsalted butter, chilled
75 g (2 1/2 oz) caster sugar
1 egg, lightly beaten

1 In a large bowl, sift together the flour, salt and cocoa powder. Cut the butter into 1 cm (1/2 inch) cubes and place in the flour. Rub the butter into the flour using your fingertips until the mixture resembles fine breadcrumbs.

2 Stir in the sugar and make a well in the centre. Pour in the egg and 1 tablespoon cold water and slowly work the mixture together using a palette knife or pastry scraper until it forms a rough ball. If it is slightly sticky, add a little more flour. Add a little more water if the pastry is too dry.

3 Turn out onto a lightly floured cool surface, gather the dough into a ball and flatten it slightly. Wrap in plastic wrap and place in the refrigerator to chill for 20 minutes before using.

Chef's tip This quantity of pastry is sufficient to line two shallow 18–20 cm (7–8inch) flan tins. If only making one flan or tart, divide the pastry into two and wrap separately in plastic wrap. Use one piece and put the second one in a plastic bag and seal, airtight, to freeze and use on another occasion.

Rub the butter into the flour, salt and cocoa powder until the mixture resembles fine breadcrumbs.

Add the egg and cold water to the mixture.

Work the mixture together with a palette knife or pastry scraper, adding a little more flour or water if necessary.

Turn the rough ball out onto a cool surface, gather into a ball and flatten slightly.

Making caramel

Dissolving your sugar in water gives a greater degree of control for caramel-making.

Place the caster sugar and water in a heavy-based pan. Fill a shallow pan with cold water and set it next to the stove.

Stir over low heat to dissolve the sugar. To prevent sugar crystals from forming, brush down the sides of the pan with a brush dipped in water.

Bring to the boil and simmer until the caramel takes on a deep golden colour. Swirl the pan to stop the caramel colouring unevenly.

Stop the cooking by plunging the bottom of the pan into the cold water for a few seconds.

Making a base for a mousse

Make sure that the sugar syrup does not become too hot or it will begin to thicken.

Whisk the egg whites until they form soft peaks.

Gradually pour half the hot sugar syrup in a fine stream onto the egg whites between the whisk and the bowl, whisking continuously, and continue whisking until cold.

Repeat this process with the remaining sugar syrup and the egg yolks, by first beating the egg yolks until they are thick and pale, then pouring on the hot sugar syrup and beating until cold.

Making lines with a skewer

Be very careful when heating and handling the skewer.

To make lines of caramel on a surface dusted with icing sugar, heat a skewer until very hot and lay it on the sugared surface briefly.

Published in 2000 by Merehurst Limited, Ferry House, 51–57 Lacy Road, Putney, London SW15 1PR.

Murdoch Books and Le Cordon Bleu would like to express their gratitude to the 42 masterchefs of all the Le Cordon Bleu Schools, whose knowledge and expertise have made this book possible, especially: Chef Terrien, Chef Boucheret, Chef Deguignet, Chef Duchêne (MOF), Chef Guillut, Chef Pinaud, Chef Cros, Paris; Chef Males, Chef Walsh, Chef Power, Chef Carr, Chef Paton, Chef Poole-Gleed, Chef Wavrin, Chef Thivet, London; Chef Chantefort, Chef Jambert, Chef Hamasaki, Chef Honda, Chef Paucod, Chef Okuda, Chef Lederf, Chef Peugeot, Chef Mori, Tokyo; Chef Salambien, Chef Boutin, Chef Harris, Sydney; Chef Lawes, Adelaide; Chef Guiet, Chef Denis, Chef Petibon, Chef Poncet, Ottawa; Chef Martin, Mexico; Chef Camargo, Brazil.
A special mention to graduate Saori Matsuma, who helped the chefs test each recipe. A very special acknowledgment to Helen Barnard, Alison Oakervee and Deepika Sukhwani, who have been responsible for the coordination of the Le Cordon Bleu team throughout this series under the Presidency of André J Cointreau.

Series Manager: Kay Halsey
Series Concept, Design and Art Direction: Juliet Cohen
Food Editor: Lulu Grimes
Designer: Michelle Cutler
Photographer: Brett Danton
Food Stylist: Marie-Hélène Clauzon
Food Preparation: Kerrie Mullins
Chef's Techniques Photographer: Reg Morrison
Home Economists: Kerrie Mullins, Kate Murdoch, Margot Smithyman, Maria Villegas

Creative Director: Marylouise Brammer
CEO & Publisher: Anne Wilson

ISBN 1 85391 980 2

Printed by Toppan Printing Hong Kong Co. Ltd. PRINTED IN CHINA
First Printed 2000
©Design and photography Murdoch Books® 2000
©Text Le Cordon Bleu 2000
All rights reserved. No part of this publication may be reproduced, stored in a retrieval system or transmitted in any form or by any means, electronic, mechanical, photocopying, recording or otherwise without the prior written permission of the publisher.

A catalogue record for this book is available from the British Library.

Distributed in the UK by D Services, 6 Euston Street, Freemen's Common, Leicester LE2 7SS Tel 0116-254-7671 Fax 0116-254-4670.
Distributed in Canada by Whitecap (Vancouver) Ltd, 351 Lynn Avenue, North Vancouver, BC V7J 2C4 Tel 604-980-9852 Fax 604-980-8197 or Whitecap (Ontario) Ltd, 47 Coldwater Road, North York, ON M3B 1Y8 Tel 416-444-3442 Fax 416-444-6630
Published and distributed in Australia by Murdoch Books®, GPO Box 1203, Sydney NSW 1045

Front cover: Fruit tartlets and Apricot and ginger shortbreads

IMPORTANT INFORMATION

CONVERSION GUIDE

1 cup = 250 ml (8 fl oz)
1 Australian tablespoon = 20 ml (4 teaspoons)
1 UK tablespoon = 15 ml (3 teaspoons)

NOTE: We have used 20 ml tablespoons. If you are using a 15 ml tablespoon, for most recipes the difference will be negligible. For recipes using baking powder, gelatine, bicarbonate of soda and flour, add an extra teaspoon for each tablespoon specified.

CUP CONVERSIONS—DRY INGREDIENTS

1 cup flour, plain or self-raising = 125 g (4 oz)
1 cup sugar, caster = 250 g (8 oz)
1 cup breadcrumbs, dry = 125 g (4 oz)

IMPORTANT: Those who might be at risk from the effects of salmonella food poisoning (the elderly, pregnant women, young children and those suffering from immune deficiency diseases) should consult their GP with any concerns about eating raw eggs.